I0149160

Freedom Time
Chosen Ones

GODDESS RAVIN NICOLE

COPYRIGHT © 2023

ALL RIGHTS RESERVED.

The contents of this book may not be reproduced, duplicated or transmitted without direct written permission from the author.

Under no circumstances will any legal responsibility or blame be held against the author or publisher for any reparation, damages or monetary loss due to the information herein, either directly or indirectly.

Legal Notice:

You cannot amend, distribute, sell, use, quote or paraphrase any part or the content within this book without the consent of the author.

Disclaimer Notice:

Please note the information contained within this document is for educational and entertainment purposes only. No warranties of any kind are expressed or implied. Readers acknowledge that the author is not engaging in rendering or legal, financial, medical or professional advice. Please consult a licensed professional before attempting any techniques outlined in this book.

By reading this document, the reader agrees that under no circumstances are is the author responsible for any losses, direct or indirect, which are incurred as a result of information contained within this document, including, but not limited to, errors. Omissions, or inaccuracies.

TABLE OF CONTENTS

The Default Program

When you were born, you were placed in the Default Program. This program is created and sustained by the "magicians behind the curtains." These are the ones who pull the strings, manipulating and influencing everything in the world around you. They want you to believe that your life is random and that you're just a tiny speck in a vast universe, with no purpose, power, or control. This ideology is designed to keep you confused, lost, asleep and blinded to your true inherent power.

The Default Program is where the illusions and lies begin. It starts when you are born and it's the beginning stage of the minds programming . This is also where lessons, challenges, and obstacles, first accumulate, some can be hard, unbearable, yet you can overcome them.

Within this Default Program, one experiences low-vibrational emotions: hurt, pain, fear, sadness, insecurity, guilt, and shame, to name a few. These low-vibrational emotions emerge from the challenges and lessons you encountered as a child. Also, childhood can involve traumas such as neglect, abandonment, physical abuse, verbal or emotional abuse, or sexual abuse. If left unhealed, these emotions and traumatic experiences can carry into your adulthood, and begin the shaping and molding of your reality. And when the inner-child is unhealed the inner-child will wreak havoc in your adulthood.

However, the truth is, you are a powerful co-creator of your reality. You are constantly shaping and molding your experiences in your reality, whether consciously or unconsciously. The "magicians behind the curtains," who pull the strings, understand this process perfectly and capitalize on your trauma, pain, and fear, whether that be from childhood or your adulthood. This is why they are constantly keeping you and the masses in a low-vibrational state. They are consistent with manipulating lives within the Default Program. Especially, those that don't know any better or who think the reality presented to them is all it is, and that it's nothing outside of that.

They know that human consciousness co-creates reality, or at least the reality presented to them, based on what is inputted into their minds. So, they will leverage this information and use it as power against people by controlling the information input. This is why they continuously to project low-vibrational energies and frequencies out into the environment and to the masses, keeping everyone in a low-vibrational emotional and mental state. So, that you don't awaken and start to create your Heaven on Earth.

One primary method they use is television. It "tell lies to your vision." They use all media outlets: news, social media, TV programs, and your favorite entertainers. This is why it's called enter-tain-ment, it enters and tains (corrupts) the mental. It's planting negative seeds in your mind and keeping you stuck on a hamster wheel going nowhere but in circles. Once the seeds are planted, people tend to water them themselves, by continuing to allow this false programming and conditioning of their mind. When the mind is hijacked the body will definitely follow.

This is why it's crucial to heal your childhood and adulthood trauma and see through the programming, conditioning, the lies and illusions you have been shown and taught. These include the false beliefs about yourself that were projected onto you, often by the systems within the Default Program that's designed to keep you trapped. And keep in mind these false narratives, illusions, and lies are constantly broad-cast, through these "black boxes," which means they're effectively casting spells through their "paid programming," unbeknownst to the masses, programming everyone's mind to help create the reality they desire for all, or the emotional or metal state they want to keep everyone, including you trapped in. You are paying for this, mentally, emotionally, spiritually, physically, vibrationally, energetically, and financially, by subscribing to it, and allowing it to continue to distort your reality. This is known as spiritual warfare and psychological warfare.

Their objective is to keep you and everyone in fear, or in a constant fight- or- flight survival mode ceasing to grow outside of the conditions set forth . This is because fear, anxiety, and stress are low-vibrational states that perfectly aligns with their agenda. By keeping you preoccupied with the unseen tactics they use and create, prevents you from rising to higher frequencies of awareness.

And challenging the reality they've constructed for you. So, they divert your energy and attention away from your inherent power.

Therefore, you must release fear and inner-stand its acronym: False Evidence Appearing Real, and reclaim your inherent power. Heal your trauma to overcome these internal and external forces/battles, and stop falling for the illusions and low vibrations, designed to snatch your power and keep you under control.

But beyond these tactics lies an even more corrupt reality, the Slave Program. Which continuously feeds you narratives, teaching you shame and self-hate. This program often leads you to self-destruct, and hating on your own reflections by behaving like "crabs in a bucket." Instead of uplifting and helping one another.

Or the American Dream Program, that also keeps you stuck on the hamster wheel in the Default Program, while participating in a rat race designed for you to never win. You are co-creators so create.

And be aware of the toxic family program that helps keep you in the "Underworld," also known as the Default Program. Unconsciously, time-looping the same cycles and toxicity.

Last, but not least, the School Program, that trains you to be an employee and teaches you to comply and conform to the systems and structures they have created for you. It also deactivates your free-thinker processor, critical thinking, and creativity. It shuts down your true gifts, talents, skills, abilities, and imagination. Over-stand that your imagination fuels your creativity, giving you the power to program your own mind and create your own reality. If you are not creating your own reality someone else will, and this is exactly what has been happening to you, especially in the Default Program. Someone else has been creating your reality for you.

You must remember that you are a spiritual being inside this "meat suit" having a human experience. You are a co-creator with the Divine and have the power within you to control how this experience unfolds. Be aware of your actions and what you feed your mind and spirit. Be mindful of negative repetitive thoughts and programs that keep you in a low vibratory mental state.

In short, many other programs exist that I haven't mention. But if you have "the eye to see" and want to see, you will. And as the scripture goes, "Many are called, but few are chosen."

So, listen, you must heal, learn your lessons, reprogram your mind, raise your vibration and rise from this lower level of existence. Don't get stuck in the Default Program. You have to heal and learn to discern the lies and misinformation that you've been shown and taught.

Remember, the moment you decide to break free from the Default Program, you'll begin to change the trajectory of your life and create your own future. By consciously choosing your own path, thoughts, beliefs, vibration, and emotions. By doing this you break-free from the false programming, lies, and illusions and replace them with the truths that aligns with your higher self. And this isn't only about counteracting external forces; it's about reclaiming your internal landscape and terminating programs that hinders your growth. And this requires courage, self-awareness, and the willingness to confront uncomfortable truths and false realities about yourself and the world around you. And when you begin to pull back the layers of the programming and conditioning, you'll begin to discover a sense of liberation and alignment with your higher-self. Allowing you to transcend lower timelines and live authentically as you continue own your Soul's Journey.

<u>Hell aka The Underworld</u>

Hell, also known as the underworld, is the belly of the beast. This cesspool is ran by malevolent forces and dark entities that roam aimlessly, trapped in their own mental anguish. It's their playground, full of toxicity, where they feel powerful and in charge. These dark entities worship the malevolent forces they serve and the dark reality it presents. They fuel their energy and ego by emotionally, verbally, spiritually, mentally, physically and financially abusing you and others. Inflicting harm onto others empowers them.

However, the Divine sends Chosen Ones into this underworld, hiding them in plain sight. They act as a catalyst for change, while the Divine use them to expose and to weigh the hearts of others. These Chosen Ones are there to shed light upon the darkness and spread love and hope towards the dark entities roaming in the dark abyss. But these dark entities are so evil, and jealous and envious of the Chosen One's light that it blinds them from seeing beyond the darkness. These dark entities will try to break the Chosen One's spirit, which in turn makes it easy for the malevolent forces they serve, to try and attach themselves to the Chosen Ones. So, the Chosen Ones must be careful and see through the traps. These dark entities will gamble with the Chosen Ones' lives and attempt to steal or swap their destiny, just as they have gambled with their own lives and destinies. However, the Chosen Ones are divinely guided and divinely protected. Every ill intent these dark entities try to bring against them will fail, as long as the Chosen Ones continue to operate and live righteously.

Furthermore, these dark entities assumed they had power over the Chosen Ones and that the Chosen Ones were weak. But it was all an illusion a test orchestrated by the Divine. The Divine allowed them to believe this, even the malevolent forces they serve knew the truth, that the Divine was always in control and holds all the power. The Divine will forever protect the Chosen Ones sent to the Underworld to help guide and lead the dark entities to the light.

Yet, these dark entities foolishly believe they can get away with their wicked ways against the Chosen Ones. They want dominance, power, and control over the Chosen One' lives when in truth, they lack power and control over their own. The demonic entities attached to them run and control their existence.

In conclusion, as the Chosen Ones go through this Underworld, their hearts will also be tested, as the scripture states, "To whom much is given, much will be required."

Lost Souls and Dark Entities

In the Underworld, there are two specific beings one will

encountered, even though there are others. These are lost souls and

dark entities. Many of these lost souls don't even realize they're lost

and asleep in the Underworld. They've been indoctrinated,

conditioned, deceived, or have demonic entities attached to them.

The trauma they've experienced plays a significant role in all of this,

keeping them from seeing the truth and piercing through the

illusions that define their existence.

The lost souls who remain oblivious and asleep are living on a

low-level dimension alongside the dark entities. They possess the

power to change if they only choose to. These lost souls are

conditioned and indoctrinated to believe someone outside

themselves will come save them from their self-destruction. They

are deeply lost and deeply confused, for they already hold

everything within them to save themselves; they simply need to tap into their own inner power. Instead, they roam lost in the abyss, inflicting self-harm and causing pain to themselves. Choosing this path over doing the necessary "shadow work" to heal their deep-rooted trauma. They neither see nor want to acknowledge the path they have fallen for or the mental hell they have created for themselves.

Then there are the dark entities who free-roam in the abyss. Due to the life choices and decisions, they have made throughout their lives. They are the ones that like to keep up a lot of devilish energy, causing destruction, chaos, and confusion. They love the dark energy that they dwell in. They are very aware that they have chosen to live in darkness and consciously chose to wreak havoc everywhere they go.

They dwell and survive in dark places, yet they think they are thriving by being in devilish energy and on "demon time." These dark entities roam in the abyss, projecting all of their inner demons, trauma, and insecurities onto others. But, as I mentioned before, they are very conscious of their behavior and actions. Don't let them fool you; It is said that the greatest trick the devil pulled was convincing the world that it didn't exist.

In closing, one must be very leery and cautious when engaging with these dark entities. These dark entities will have ill intentions for you and towards you. They possess a very dark energy and have a low vibratory mental state; and operate on a very low frequency, which keeps them in lower dimensions. And they will stop at nothing to pull you into that dark energy with them and drag you down to that low vibratory mental state of existence they dwell in.

In conclusion, energy transference is real and if you engage with them or continue for long periods, your vibration and energy will be lowered. And you'll be at risk at dwelling in that dark energy with them. So, protect your energy and keep your vibrations high; stay positive and maintain a positive mindset, especially, when you are in situations and have no choice but to deal with them. Overall, and most importantly, don't allow yourself to get sucked into their misery.

Karmic Family

Being born into the karmic family reveals a truth that can be hard for some to accept. These aren't just challenging relationships, but malicious, evil, and deceitful members of your bloodline, who literally hate your existence. They will go through extreme measures to keep you from seeing their true nature, and to keep you from walking in your purpose and power.

Their cruel acts towards you are characterized by a deep-seated hatred, and the fear of your light, purpose and power. Your light illuminates their true nature, and inner demons, which drives their inner demons; to orchestrate and create blockages designed to keep you from your purpose, trapped, disempowered, and bound to them. Their ill will against you can sometimes follow you from past life experiences. But it often stems from past behavior, unresolved trauma, or pain passed down from a previous generation. Surfacing as a relentless karmic cycle within the karmic family dynamic.

And even though you are viewed as a threat to these karmic family members. And they were continuously hurting and abusing you throughout your life; while, plotting and scheming and hoping that you'd never come out of the fog and see them for the dark entities that they are. Because their ingrained dysfunction is so deeply-rooted, and they did everything in their power to keep you under their influence, control, and asleep. While hoping they could take your light from you, and pull you into their darkness. These reasons being why they were intentionally abusing and misguiding you, for their own sick, insidious benefits.

However, it is the Divine who truly orchestrates this entire dynamic, using their very actions to trigger your Awakening and align you with your Divine Purpose. However, the dysfunctionality within them, though designed to prevent your Awakening and hinder your Divine Purpose, eventually, becomes the very thing that triggers your Awakening. And when someone like you came along and threaten their entire existence, it becomes unfathomable for them. And when the manipulation tactics, gaslighting, and dark magic they were doing and using against you to keep you in the fog, cease to affect you any longer, is when your healing journey begins.

They know that you are the Divine Chosen One, sent to break the generational curses placed on your bloodline. So, while these relationships can be challenging, they're there to be a catalyst to your Spiritual Awakening, healing, and self-development. And through this karmic family dynamic, vital life lessons are learned, such as self-love, setting firm boundaries, discerning true intentions, cultivating resilience, and unwavering strength. This very personal transformation, forged through these very trials, will align you with your higher purpose and prepare you for the next phase of your life's journey.

Furthermore, by you consciously choosing to heal, and move forward, and leave the past behind, you're not only saving your life but also the generations coming after you. So, learn your lessons and move on. You cannot change people. People have to want change for themselves. And you can't change the family you were born into. But maybe one day, they'll want better for themselves, and will do the necessary inner work to bring on that change.

Generational Curses

Generational curses are unresolved trauma, negative patterns/experiences, negative entities/energies, struggles or burdens, or limiting beliefs, that are passed down from one generation to the next when gone unhealed or unaddressed. These curses can consist of many of things: alcohol abuse, drug abuse, domestic violence, mental illness, rape or molestation, broken families, poverty, karmic debt, emotional wounds, unlearned lessons etc.

These curses can go unhealed or/and unaddressed for many generations. In most cases, the Chosen One, also known as the Black Sheep/Rebel, is sent to be the curse/cycle breaker and family healer of these curses in order to heal their bloodline.

The Chosen One does this by calling out the dysfunctional behavior within the family system. They'll speak the unspoken truths and expose the family secrets, past and present struggles and burdens, and unhealed trauma that the others would like to keep buried. They are the catalyst for change, which forces the family system to confront the uncomfortable realities. They will challenge the family norms, rules, and truths, and naturally reject the dysfunction and refuse to conform. They see the underlying generational curses and dysfunction.

They perceive reality differently, even if they are misunderstood, and labeled the outcast by the others. However, they are the one who paves the way for future generations, showing them that there are different healthier ways of living and that anything is possible.

In conclusion, even though the Chosen One might take on a lot of the family's burdens, emotional struggles/dumping and generational curses of the family system in order to heal and transmute that energy. They are also the way-shower who is the courageous disruptor of it all.

Chosen One

The Chosen One's path is rarely smooth but it's a transformative journey with a significant Soul Purpose related to their ancestral lineage. They absorb and process the emotional and energetic residue of their past and present generations. They are the Divine, Chosen One.

They are viewed or considered the black sheep, outcast, or oddball in their dysfunctional family dynamic; however, they couldn't fit in even if they tried. They sometimes feel lonely despite being surrounded by people, or are forced into isolation for not conforming to their family's toxicity. They are very different, misunderstood, critically judged, mocked, or met with resistance or anger, for their life choices, beliefs, or lifestyle that deviates from the dysfunction of their toxic family norm.

They are often overlooked and mistreated by those that they love and are loyal to. They are often emotionally manipulated, blamed, scapegoated, and projected on for their toxic family's emotional baggage and unaddressed trauma/issues. They are deceived and manipulated by family members and those close to them that use manipulation tactics like guilt to prevent them from setting boundaries, despite them being loyal to a fault. They are often met with resistance, anger, or punished with ostracism or forced isolation, emotional cut-offs, for challenging the family's toxic system/behavior. Their feelings, experiences, or perception are often invalidated, dismissed or denied by those close to them. No one wants to acknowledge the Chosen One's value until the Chosen One separate themselves from all the toxicity that goes on within their toxic family dynamic or relationships.

And when this occurs, the Chosen One begin to have an internal shift or shift in perception. The impact of the traumatic challenges and significant life event(s) they have endured awakens them on a different level of higher consciousness and awareness. They begin to see through the veil of illusions surrounding them or that once surrounded them. This is known as a Spiritual Awakening, and it can transpire differently for everyone.

Through this process, they begin to heal their internal and external emotional struggles, burdens, and conflicts. They step in to their healing journey with resilience, and unbreakable/unshakeable strength. They begin to tap into their profound gifts and open themselves up to deeper spiritual insights, awareness, and higher consciousness.

They begin to transcend everything that was hindering them from stepping into their power and purpose. They start to overcome all their challenges by tapping into their inner power. They start healing ancestral trauma by healing themselves while continuing to heal and navigate personal and ancestral challenges. They start forging a new path for the generations coming after them. They become leaders and catalysts for profound change.

Their presence, wisdom, knowledge, and experiences become the power to assisting with helping and healing others. They have always carried a healing energy, and their immense courage is ultimately liberating not only for themselves but their entire lineage and others.

The Empath

Empaths possess what is often described as a sixth sense. This paranormal ability allows them to intuitively grasp the emotional and mental states of others. They can also sense underlying energies, subtle cues, unspoken truths, and unspoken intentions. Guided by a powerful intuition, this makes them remarkably in tune with themselves, others, and their surroundings. They often possess a deep knowing beyond mere feelings that transcends regular logic or surface emotions.

Due to their sensitivity, empaths often dislike crowds because of the heavy emotions and energy that they absorb from others. This constant influx of absorption can be overwhelming and incredibly draining both emotionally and energetically, for the empath. Because of their naturally caring nature and ability to understand, they tend to be great problem solvers. It's common for everyone they know, including strangers, to effortlessly approach them with their difficulties. Empaths have a natural healing aura that others can feel, making people feel comfortable, talking about their problems to the empath.

However, the empath's profound sensitivity, while a gift often comes with significant personal cost. This deep attunement means they not only feel others' emotions but can struggle to distinguish them from their own. If an empath is still learning to navigate or control their gift, they might unknowingly take on others' emotions or thought-forms as if these were their own. This can lead to confusion, feeling overwhelmed, and a challenge in maintaining their own emotional clarity. While deeply empathetic, an empath's profound connection to others requires strict boundaries and sharp discernment. Without these, their tendency to absorb others' problems as their own can lead to severe self-neglect and emotional exhaustion. This vulnerability makes them susceptible to emotional dumping and the projections of others' insecurities and inner-demons, making them particularly vulnerable to "energy vampires" such as narcissists or individuals who are emotionally manipulative or constantly negative. Such interactions result in an unreciprocated energy exchange that depletes their own energy and takes a significant toll on their mental and emotional well-being.

So, empaths often have a need to decompress and recharge from absorbing others' energies, frequently, needing solitude and quiet environments to restore and balance their own energy.

In conclusion, Empaths, some being Chosen Ones, have a profound connection to the world around them. This remarkable characteristic trait and unique powerful gift, and their expansive hearts, gives them the ability to feel the suffering of others, and propels them to extend help to anyone in need. This inherent nature and gift shapes their unique journey and shows their vital importance as an individual who is the embodiment of love, kindness, and compassion, even amidst a world that has been desensitized. Their unique journey often calls for them to be that beacon of light, one who inspires others, to be more loving, kind, and compassionate towards themselves and others.

The Narcissist

Be aware of the Narcissist. This evil, dark being comes to steal, kill, and destroy. They are experts at manipulating, lying, and deceiving others. They will literally have you feeling like you are trapped in a prison, except its mental. And it's a prison they have created for you. They have one agenda towards their victims and that is to usurp their energy. By constantly manipulating and abusing them to fuel their own energy, then leaving them depleted of their energy. Which will have their victims feeling tired and drained emotionally, mentally, spiritually, and physically. One have to learn how to identify these "energy vampires." They are wolves in sheep clothing, the trickster spirit. They are weak and insecure, and jealous and envious of their victims; and only want to cause them harm. They will mishandle them and use them up, until they think it's nothing left for them but death.

So, stay watchful and mindful of these evil spirits that roam and hide behind their shell. They will hurt you and beat you down verbally, emotionally, physically, mentally, spiritually, and financially. They will use all kinds of methods and tactics in order to disarm, misuse, and confuse you. Leaving you with no energy or mental clarity to defend and protect yourself. They experts at playing mind games. Don't allow your judgement to become cloudy, when engaging with these demons. They serve a malevolent force, and their darkness has come; to try and overpower and devour your light. That godly force that resides within you. These entities are sent by the devil to destroy and distract you from your soul purpose and soul-evolution, or to teach you vital life-changing lessons.

And they will do everything in their sick mind to diminish you. They'll love bomb you in order to disarm you. Then, they'll eventually start to manipulate, gaslight, devalue, then discard you.

They have a cycle that they hope you won't ever catch on to or recognize. So be very discerning and observant around these demons. They are cold-hearted, very toxic, and will try to keep you trapped in their unhealthy toxic cycle. And when people cannot manipulate you, they'll call you crazy or tell others you're crazy; or just get to lying to people about you. And when or if that don't work, they'll role switch; and try to play the victim and make you out to be the abuser.

So, be mindful of them and their manipulation tactics, because narcissistic people only want control over your life; and to feed off of your energy because they are dead on the inside. Be very careful cause this can and will have a detrimental effect on your health and psyche. Learn your lessons and RUN!!! Do not get stuck on the hamster wheel with them. These people will not change. They only change victims.

<u>The Dark Empath</u>

The Dark Empath, also known as dark witches and dark warlocks. Share some of the same traits of a narcissist, if not all; and vice versa. These malevolent dark evil entities are truly insidious. These beings are aware of the emotions and vulnerabilities of others. But they do not feel those emotions themselves. And they absolutely have no empathy or sympathy for you. But they will use what they know as a calculated weapon to manipulate and exploit others.

They only seek to manipulate, exploit, and destroy others, for their own personal gains. They have a mental illness and a low, deep-rooted lack of self-worth. They have a dark sense of humor and will exploit you when giving the opportunity. They will spiritually attack you and have you in a constant state of spiritual battle, if you continue to associate with them. They live in a constant state of misery and bitterness. And they want you to as well.

They are a predators and assessors for the devil. They watch and they study you and learn your weaknesses, in order to use them against you. Do not trust these malevolent beings. They lurk in the darkness hoping not to be seen. While using dark magic to control and manipulate you, with hopes of overpowering you.

Be very cautious around these malevolent beings. They will do all kinds of dark magic and spells to get you to turn and not trust in the Divine. They might even try to kill you or get you to kill yourself. So, you'll need the strength and the armor of protection from the Divine to defeat these malevolent beings. You will not be able to do it alone. You'll be no match for this wicked energy. If you ever have to go up against one of these dark entities walk in faith, and not by sight. And keep your discernment on full blast.

Twin Flame

A Twin Flame, relationship is all about igniting growth within each other and it's a Divine Union. Your twin flame will mirror your behavior in order to show you where you need growth and where change is needed. Not everyone has a twin flame connection. But if you do buckle up. This connection can be very magnetic and intense. It is said that a twin flame relationship is a soul split in two.

So, you will automatically feel a strong connection to this person. And it don't have to be a romantic relationship.

However, this connection comes with a lot of challenges and rewards. This connection will teach you to value and love yourself unconditionally. It will also teach you to heal those parts of yourself that needs healing. Twin Flames, relationships usually involves, the runner and the chaser. And these roles can switch between the two of you throughout the relationship.

This happens out of the fear of growth and the fear of accepting the level of deep connection you two share. And this can be scary for some. But if you stick it out you will learn self-love, self-growth and self-discovery. This will be a profound personal transformation for the both of you.

False Twin Flame

The false twin flame comes in love bombing you and mirroring your behavior. So, you will start to think that they are the love of your life and that you all have so much in common. But that is all an illusion, once you see their mask slip and see their true colors. Then, you'll see that demon for what it really is. They are a narcissist at best.

They have been deceiving you since you first encountered them. You might have even rejected them or overlooked them in the past, prior to dating them. And they remember that experience and how that experience felt to them and how they were emotionally and mentally wounded by it.

And more than likely, you didn't know how they felt about that first experience between you two and had no ill intentions behind it.

You just weren't interested in dating or having a relationship with them. So, they came in with a hidden agenda to make you feel that exact same way that they felt when they first approached you.

They might have even been stalking you before making that first, contact with you. They are very much like the narcissist, a predator. The false twin flame also known as the karmic partner are very calculated and malicious. They are very skilled at manipulating and targeting their victims.

Just like a narcissist their victims of choice are empaths. And their energy signature is dark and cold. Very devilish and vampiric. They will drain you of your energy and try to pull the life force out of you. They will try to keep you in a state of confusion and abuse you in all degrees, just as a narcissist. They will do all kinds of dark magic, including word magic to keep you under their spells. Be aware and stay alert of these lurking dark entities. Once you break free from

under their spells and illusions, get out, immediately, and stay out.

Or they will diminish your light and spirit.

<u>Sex Magic</u>

Magic can be used for good or evil. One of the forms of magic these dark entities use is called Sex Magic. The energy behind it is very devilish, lustful, fiery, and can be very alluring.

This is the narcissist most often used form of dark magic. They use it to reel you in and keep you bound to them. They do this by sending you sexual thought-forms or by thinking sexual thoughts about you when they are around you or away from you. And if you don't have discernment, you might think that energy or them thoughts are that of your own.

This is known as energy manipulation. It don't always have to involve sex. They can still send sexual energy into your electro-magnetic field. If you are not conscious of your own energy, then you will not know someone is playing in your energy field. This is an untactful way, they manipulate your energy to get you attached to them. So, they can latch onto your energy and have you contracting into a soul-tie with them.

However, they do all kinds of spells to get you and keep you locked and stuck to them. They will cast word spells onto you that keep you under their dark illusions. So, you must be aware of these energies that's trying to bind you to them and get you to conform to their dark ways.

Also, once you have sex with them, you're going to be interconnected with them and all of their traumas and low vibrating energies. That's why it's called Sex also known as Sexual Energy Xchange.

You'll begin to take on their insecurities and their lack of self-worth. Then you'll start vibrating on low level frequencies that keep you stuck in a lower timeline with them. So, you cannot continue to exchange your sexual energy with these dark entities. It will also stop your creativity and drain you of your own essence, and give it to them. Now, you are unable to create like you were before you started engaging in sexual activities with these demons. They'll drain you of your life force and leave you feeling depleted. And you will notice the change. They are constantly projecting all of their darkness onto you and stealing your creativity and light.

Sexual Energy Xchange is like Sacred Energy Xchange, for some. And when you carry this kind of sacred energy you cannot be exchanging your energy with just any and everybody energy signature. That's how STD's (Sexually Transmitted Demons), get passed to sacred people.

You must treat your body like the temple it is. And not allow just anyone into your womb. Or if you're a male you cannot just be spreading your sacred semen to just anyone. These dark entities are out here lurking and looking for sacred energy to devour. So, be very mindful of those that you give parts of yourself to. It can become

very damaging for your wellbeing, very quickly.

Isolation

Isolation can feel very lonely and tormenting but inner-stand that the changes you must go through in order to free yourself from all forms of bondage requires this. This is a scary phase for freeing yourself from all the programming that have been installed in your conscious and subconscious. And from energies that have been attached to you and keeping you from being aligned with your higher-self. You must become aware of all these things that has kept you attached to them whether that was out of fear or lack of knowledge of self.

However, deep inner cosmic surgery is needed. You are being isolated so the Divine, and your divine spiritual team can work on you. You're going to get this deep cleansing that is deprogramming your mind and healing your mind, body, and soul. And releasing you from attachments that are are no longer serving your higher-self.

And while you're going through this major operation, your awareness and anxiety is heighten. Your whole world, better yet, what you were led to believe was your whole world, is crumbling down. You'll start to see the mental, emotional, and verbal manipulation/abuse for what it truly was. And you'll realize you have been misrepresenting yourself. And you have allowed others to you mishandle, misguide, gas-light, manipulate, use, and abuse you. And most of the times, it's by those that you have loved and trusted.

And although betrayal is heartbreaking and even worse when it's those you care about, however, you have to over-stand that these were roles that these people were playing in your life. They were wolves in sheep clothing. And the Divine will start to reveal all these things to you in isolation while you are healing, renewing, and being restored in your mind, body and soul.

And forgiveness is necessary, not for them but for you. So, you don't have to live life with a heavy heart, so forgive them; and release and move on from them karmic energies.

Shadow Work aka Dark Knight of the Soul

The process involving isolation requires you to go into the darkness another layer of hell, in order to come out on the other side, to the Light aka Heaven aka Christ Consciousness. And this is where mental clarity resides and it's not going to be easy, it's where you realize you have been mishandled, used, and abused etc. And how you played your part in all of this, it's the raw and hardcore truth.

And it's very lonely and daunting, but if you put in the work and start to face your own inner demons and shadows. And begin to heal those wounds that have been laying there dormant unhealed. Your spirit will become lighter, your vision clearer and the fog will dissipate.

But you must face yourself, and most people are scared to do this, but shadow work requires this. Working on your unconscious mind and exploring your inner darkness or shadow self to uncover the parts of yourself that you repress and hide from can be challenging and uncomfortable. But you must take that leap of faith and look at all of you, flaws and all by diving deep within self to get to the roots of the traumas, feelings and behavior. You must see where you were powerless and how you gave your power away. This is how you gain your power back and live authentically.

Also, the Divine will begin to unveil things to you, and you will remember your pain and suffering and it will hurt. But if you stand strong and steadfast, and be committed to your shadow work, you will prevail through the dark knight of the soul and begin to become your authentic self. Then you can start to tap into your Christ

Consciousness. But first, you must heal and release all of the

baggage that keeps you from getting to this state of mind.

Inner Child Work- Healing

This is where your healing journey truly begins. Inner child work involves nurturing and healing the parts of your younger self wounded by your upbringing and early life experiences. Your younger version likely felt, lost, scared, and in pain. To mend these deep wounds, you must nurture both your inner child and your current self with self-love, self-care, self-respect, self-discipline, and self-validation.

Most adults struggle with childhood wounds, and a dysregulated nervous system, often displaying behavior that stems early on from their childhood dysfunction, such as abandonment issues, neglect, psychological or emotional abuse, physical abuse, or witnessing domestic violence and substance abuse within their family.

And childhood trauma can have a very negative effect on a person's life and overall well-being. Because your younger self plays a major role in your adulthood, influences your life choices and the decisions you have made throughout life. And if you don't heal those childhood wounds, you'll continue to time-loop and repeat the same lessons and cycles until you face them.

So, you must heal and recover from it, truly over-standing and inner-standing where growth and healing are needed.

Furthermore, if left unhealed, these patterns can tragically repeat and influence how one raises their own children. So, to truly heal and stop these cycles and curses from repeating to the next generation, you must gain clarity, confront the battles you've faced, and release them to the Divine for healing and transmutation.

Lay Your Burdens Down

You must allow the Divine to help you free yourself from these entities and energies that have/had a stronghold on you. It's the only way for deep, internal healing and true deliverance. So much has happened since you were born into this world and you need healing. So many traumas has carried on from your childhood into your adulthood. And you need a deep cleansing. The Divine will heal all of your suffering and give you inner peace. It's a process and not something that happens overnight. But you will see the changes as you commit and stay consistent to your healing journey and serving your higher purpose.

Those that choose not to heal their wounds and childhood trauma finds themselves escaping and numbing their pain with drugs, alcohol or sex etc. So, you must face your fears and heal to avoid those addictions or to overcome those addictions.

Once you do you will be renewed, restored, and transformed. But you must start to love and value yourself wholeheartedly. You are worthy of the Divine unconditional love. Know that your life have meaning and you have a divine purpose that is a part of the bigger macro cosmic plan.

You have a soul mission that needs to be fulfilled. And it requires the healed version of yourself. There are many layers that you must uncover and shed about yourself and heal those wounds that has traumatically impacted and hindered you for so long.

So don't rush the process but be committed and consisted to the process. Self-growth is important for your soul's evolution, and you are healing from this lifetime and many of others. And when you start to heal, you start to heal your bloodline.

The Healing Journey

For this deep internal healing to occur, you'll need to allow the Divine, to assist you along your healing journey. This assistance is crucial to freeing you from all the restraints and constraints that has held you captive, preventing you from your healing, self-growth, self-discovery, self-transformation, and the ability to love yourself unconditionally.

The healing journey is an individual task and can be very lonely. Since the day you were born, you've experienced numerous traumas, forming different trauma bonds with different people. These bonds often stems from the trauma itself, or from an inherent familial connection. But to gain true inner peace, you must heal and release yourself from these attachments by intentionally releasing and disconnecting from them with love.

The Divine said that all our suffering will end once we turn back to the Divine. This means you need to turn back to yourself and start loving and valuing you. Pour back into you. This isn't an easy or overnight task; it takes time and dedication to achieve the benefits from working on healing all of your traumas. And I can guarantee that you will start to see those changes if you stay consistent and committed to your healing journey. You'll begin to see how dead weight leaves your life effortlessly and how multiple personal transformations occur daily. Throughout this journey, you'll experience many deaths and rebirths of self for the new version of you to emerge. But to truly embark on this path, you must choose yourself first. Start to forgive, love, and value yourself. Know that you are worthy of all the good that life has to offer you, including the unconditional love of the Divine Spirit.

And remember that you came into this life with a Divine Soul Mission and Soul Purpose. Each layer that you discover about yourself requires the shedding of parts that no longer serve your higher self. Different versions of you will emerge as the old fades away. This isn't a process you can rush; you're unlearning and relearning many programs you thought you knew about the world, its people, and yourself. And you are healing from many lifetimes, facing and healing, unhealed traumas carried into this lifetime from the past. Simultaneously, along with the traumas created here, and generational traumas that has been passed down. Take it easy on yourself and stay in the present moment, allowing things to just unfold naturally and just flow.

Self-Love and Self Care

Self-love and Self-care requires you to put yourself, first. You must be your first priority before anything outside of yourself. And that's not being selfish but a requirement when you embark on this journey. You have to overcome the people pleasing trauma response and stop over-extending yourself where your energy is not reciprocated. And establishing strong boundaries and having the courage to say "No" when you don't want to do something that is out of alignment with where you are in the present moment. And by nurturing your own mind, body, and soul. By staying grounded and catering to your own emotional and mental well-being. Nourishing, and pouring into yourself before another. By pouring into your own cup before someone else's, your cup will have an overflow, and you can then pour into others without emptying your own cup. You must keep your own soul replenished and full. And be aware when you need to take a step back and not overwhelm yourself with things outside of yourself.

And you must be okay with putting yourself first. When you're not putting yourself first, you're taking from your own cup and neglecting yourself. And at risk to your cup running low. Which usually happens when you allow others to take from your cup without pouring back into you, leaving you depleted and empty. And this leads back to the road of self-destruction, self-sabotage, and self-neglect. You must take accountability for yourself and allow others to do the same for themselves. So, if something is being taking from your cup or you giving from your cup, and it's not being reciprocated in some way shape or form, then remove yourself physically, mentally, emotionally, and energetically.

You must start to value yourself and your inner-peace. And if something is jeopardizing this, you must be okay with doing what's best for you. Pour into those that pour into you. And only allow

those around you that value your time, presence, and energy. This is

how you start your self-love and self-care journey.

Detaching Through Self-Love

When you begin to love and heal yourself and are taking good care of yourself, physically, emotionally, mentally, and spiritually, people you were once close to will notice this positive change with you. They'll also noticed the manipulation tactics they used to use on you; will no longer work on you. So, you must keep your discernment on full blast, your vibrations high, and continue on your self-love and self-care journey. And do not allow these lower-level vibrating entities back into your life, as their negativity will only hinder your progress. And your journey of self-discovery, personal transformation, and Soul's evolution requires a supportive and positive environment that's based off connections not attachments.

And despite their realization that you're no longer susceptible to their deception and illusions, and that you're starting to love yourself and detach from codependence with people who don't have your best interests at heart and that don't love and value you. Trust and believe these individuals will still react negatively and try to gaslight you or whatever they come up with to try and disarm and derail you.

And as you become more aware of yourself and identify those who aren't good for your growth and well-being, the time will come for you to cut off all access points to you. And they'll be upset that you're no longer available or reachable. But now, you see through their games and deceit so the program will terminate. No more draining you of your good positive uplifting energy, because you see them for who they truly are, despite any title that once bound you to them. Plus, your energy won't fulfill them in ways that it used to. It's not the same satisfaction they once received from abusing you to siphon your energy. However, they'll continue to try and blindside you to get you back as one of their primary fuel sources. They'll try to gaslight you as I mentioned earlier, attempting to make you question your reality and actions in a last-ditch effort to pull you back under their illusionary spells. Because their reality is crumbling without your positive energy to feed off. Or they will try to love-bomb you, but be warned, it's a setup, do not fall for it.

When you learn where you stand in a person's life, make them stand on it. That's what self-love and self-care is all about, taking care of yourself without regret. But be wise, do what's best for you. Have discernment and use your intuition; it's your inner navigation compass, a gift from Spirit.

Personal Transformation

Self-love, self-care, and self-growth, comes with a lot of goodbyes. You must be willing to cut ties by letting go and releasing soul ties that are attached to you, but are no longer serving your higher purpose, and step into the unknown. It's a requirement when choosing yourself and walking away from anything hindering you from elevating and moving into the next phase of your life. Sacrifices have to be made if you want better for yourself and a better life. You must be willing to walk away from the familiarities and things you are attached to and have become accustomed to, without being afraid of the unknown. Venturing into unfamiliar territory is frightening but know they are opportunities for growth. And embracing the unknown will lead you to personal transformations.

This can be very complicated, and you might feel sad, confused, and overwhelmed. After all, you're leaving behind the only life you knew existed and the people you love, and that you thought loved you too.

This can appear to be a very difficult challenge, but if you want to do better, and you know better, you'll do better, and make the transition. The life you are leaving behind was an illusion; it was not real. And while the experiences were real, the people you were experiencing were taking advantage of you and deceiving you. Now the time has come for you to live a more authentic life, building solid connections, and being surrounded by people that truly love, value, and care for your well-being. What you've experienced with those people who manipulated and took advantage of your kindness, mistaking it for weakness, is now your strength. You must have the courage to move on, fully equipped with the information you've discovered about both them and yourself. This is essential for a new life to emerge, one that is in better alignment with who you are. To do this, you must leave the old one behind. You cannot change the family that you were born into to learn your earthly lessons, but what you can do is create the life that you want, a life that is truly fulfilling for you on a soul-evolutionary level.

Once you learn the lessons that you needed from your experiences. It will be of great benefit for you to start building healthy connections with people that love and value your divine presence. And as you are cleansed of all the negative energy that has hindered your soul growth for so long, your aura field and spirit will be renewed and restored, just as the Divine promised.

Now, your pure energy, your own unique energy signature, and high vibration can work in your favor according to the Universal laws of attraction, you truly attract what you are. However, let me add for you to have discernment with this, because if you're a

Chosen One, your presence alone attracts both good and bad

people. But if you have done the inner work, you'll be able to

distinguish the real from the fake. And you'll know what's in

alignment for you.

<u>Stepping into Your New Beginning</u>

Once you choose yourself and walk away from anything and everything that is not in alignment with who you truly are, better things will start to happen in your life. When you choose yourself, let go, and leave behind everything and anything, people, places, or things, that no longer serves your highest purpose or hinders your growth and progression, you open the door to a better life. And you are the co-creator of that life.

However, you must be willing to walk away from your old life without fear or any doubt. Even though this can be hard you must persevere, in order to step into a new life that aligns with your higher self.

Over-stand that the people you're leaving behind only liked and tolerated the asleep and unhealed version of you. Now, that you have Awaken, and walking in your truths and purpose. Things will never go back to being the same. And as, Newton's Third Law of Motion states, "To move forward, you have to leave something behind." And if you want to propel forward, everything and everybody cannot go with you. So, you must accept and let all of that go, and move on to your next level.

Inner-stand that you cannot bring hell into heaven. Don't allow any opposing forces to keep you from evolving and reaching higher heights. You must elevate to the new level without fear, if you truly want this new beginning. Don't let anyone stop you, and don't self-sabotage this opportunity. Remember, you are not obligated to sacrifice your inner and outer peace for those that who aren't at any degree of peace with themselves.

Positive Energy vs Negative Energy

Positive energy is the very essence of the Divine, a loving, high-vibrational energy. It feels peaceful, kind, compassionate, and deeply healing. Some individuals carry this divine energy signature wherever they go, and others can instantly sense it. They bring a profound sense of peace to their surroundings, and both children and animals are naturally drawn to them, instinctively recognizing their unique essence.

In contrast, negative energy is also drawn and attracting to this energy, seeking only to feed upon it. Those who carry a lower vibration typically resent the person radiating positive energy and they seek to drain it. Sometimes, their true intentions are obvious, like their words, body language, and facial expressions clearly reveal they do not vibrate on a high frequency or a frequency of love. Others might avoid them at all costs, hoping they won't detect their resentfulness and inner demons. Also, be aware of those who conceal their true intentions, for they primarily want to siphon and drain this energy. They'll give backhanded compliments or make slick remarks or engage in subtle acts with the intent to provoke or diminish the energy, and then try to hide their hand. These individuals are often in a perpetually negative mental state, and their lives are constantly plagued by negativity. You can both feel and see how low their vibrations are. They dislike seeing others in good spirits or with high vibrations, so they'll try to hurt them or pull them down to uplift themselves in hopes of siphoning their energy. This tactic can sometimes work if the person is unaware of their manipulative games.

In addition, they might find themselves feeling awkward or uneasy around these kinds of people. This is the body's innate warning system, alerting them to be cautious and aware.

It's crucial to over-stand that these dynamics can even occur with family members who project their insecurities onto you. You may experience a sense of unease when you're around them, which could signify negative energy being directed at you, or perhaps a negative attachment they carry that is irritated by your positive vibrant energy.

When you're deeply connected to yourself and truly know who you are, you'll intuitively feel their energy. You'll sense that something around you is not of the high vibration you carry. Therefore, stay attuned to your energy and vibrations. If you encounter or engage in conversation with one of these individuals and suddenly feel out of alignment, if your energy seem off or exhausted, or your vibration has dropped, and your mental state has shifted to a state that is not of your own, then you've likely been in contact with an energy vampire.

So, it's best to remove yourself from that person's presence as quickly as possible. Afterward, cleanse your energy by taking a salt bath or saging yourself and your environment. Or whatever positive reinforcement you need to do to get back in alignment.

High Vibrations vs Low Vibrations

Every moment of our lives involves the exchange of energy, often felt more than seen. For instance, the subtle shifts in your own being, the moments you feel light and uplifted, and those when a heaviness pulls you down. These aren't just random acts or moods; they are reflections of your energy and your vibrational frequencies. As well as the seen and unseen energy forces that influences your energy and vibration. Every thought, emotion, and interactions contributes to your overall energetic state, either raising you higher or pulling you lower. Over-standing and mastering your energy and vibrations is key to consciously shaping your reality.

Mastering your energy and vibrations means consistently maintaining a positive mental state, no matter your external circumstances. This isn't about ignoring challenges, but choosing to respond from a place of inner strength and inner peace. You can achieve this by consciously engaging in daily activities that nourishes your soul and spirit.

For instance, listening to positive affirmations music or reciting positive affirmations are excellent practices. Spending time out in nature, or by water can be very replenishing. Reading an inspiring book, spending time with yourself, or creating something. Or whatever high-vibrational activities you choose to uplift yourself and sustain a positive mental state, do it.

This also means avoiding people, places, and things that pull you into a negative mindset and lower your energy and vibration. Because things that lead people to a low vibrational or energy state often involve exposure to or engagement in low-vibrational energies and activities. Whether that be environments with heavy negativity, or around people who gossip and talk about others or tear them down. This low-vibrational behavior. Also, watching negative low-vibrational TV programs that contains violence or drama, that inflicts fear, despair, anger, or sadness, can pull you into a low-vibrational state and drain your energy. As well as listening to low-vibrational music, which can also draw you into a lower energetic or vibrational state. Playing violent video games can also pull you into a low-vibrational or energetic state. These kinds of exposures are detrimental to your emotional, mental, spiritual, physical, or financial well-being. These experiences and habits don't replenish your spirit or feed your soul; instead, they lower your vibration, and energy, leaving you feeling out of alignment. And being in this state, growth and evolution isn't possible. You'll find yourself repeating and recycling the same outdated experiences and outcomes day in and day out. Your actions and the people you surround yourself with will reflect this stagnation and low vibration.

However, simply put engaging with negative frequencies and destructive behaviors only have you spiraling down, instead of spiraling up.

Distractions

Distractions are anything that keeps you from tapping into self and knowing thyself. And finding out the truth of who you truly are. Which is a sovereign energy/spiritual being forever evolving. And energy can never be created or destroyed, but transformed.

However, distractions can be anything that keeps you from aligning with your higher self and tapping into your full capabilities. And that can be people, places, or things that distract you and keep you from this very notion. It can also be manipulation tactics that are used by those around you or close to you to keep you from; knowledge of self, Awakening, or for their own hidden intentions/agendas.

And keep in mind you can be a distraction/hinderance to yourself. By not acknowledging the truth and being comfortable living a lie.

For example, not healing when you know you should be facing your inner demons and traumas and healing them. Or, by avoiding things that you know your spirit is calling you to do or not to do. But instead, you ignore the promptings and distract yourself with irrelevant nonsense that keeps you on the hamster wheel. Which in return keeps you from your Divine Purpose. Just how others manipulate and distract you, to keep you from your Divine Purpose and Soul's Evolution..

Also, distractions can be anything that keeps you hidden and distracted from facing reality or in a physical or mental state time freeze. Lacking direction or clarity. That's basically, how distractions operate or set-up to keep you in a state of confusion, patterns, time loops, or karmic cycles. By keeping you stuck in unhealthy patterns, situation-ships, experiences, and circumstances.

You'll find yourself time-looping the same experiences and unwanted thoughts and emotions that make you feel lost, confused, stagnant, and not in control of yourself or your life. When in all actuality you hold the power and the ability to control and dictate your life as you want and see fit. You are the controller, and you are the operator, and navigator of your life, until you relinquish this power to something outside of yourself. But if you don't know this and just allow the internal and external programs to run and control your life then you'll stuck believing you have no control or power over yourself or life. And if you haven't learned the lessons the distractions or experiences are teaching and showing you. Then they are repeated, and you keep time-looping. Which is self-sabotaging and self-hindering to yourself.

So, you have to use your spiritual eye to see the repetitive distractions and experiences being shown to you; in the same person/people or different ones. Because the patterns, emotions, challenges will still arise and manifest in different people, experiences, and circumstances, until you learn the lesson. So, if you find yourself experiencing similar scenarios, emotions, patterns, behavior, or whatever, but with different people or with your own doings. Stop, take a step back and ask yourself, what is this trying to show or tell/teach me; there you'll find your answers. And know if it's not in alignment with who you are or what you are pursuing, then it's a distraction or a lesson needing to be learned.

So, learn your lessons and move on so you can unlock new levels. And remember just like in video games there are many distractions, blockages, and challenges put in place to keep you from achieving your goal or completing the mission. But in this case, to keep you from seeing the truth, elevating, knowing thy-self, and tapping into your inner-power and breaking free from outdated programs

behavior, and relationships that have run their course.

Blockages

Blockages are anything that keeps you confined, constrained, restrained; emotionally, mentally, spiritually, physically, and financially. This implies to people, places, and things. When something is blocking you it is creating an obstacle(s) or perceived obstacle(s) to limit or hinder you. This can also imply to something that is internally within you, such as a self-belief, lack of self-confidence, lack of motivation, self-doubt, outdated programs, negative thinking, comfort zone, emotions, just to name a few.

However, people can create blockages for you as well that keeps you from knowing thyself or information that will help liberate or elevate yourself. Or to keep you from living in bliss on your divine path, exercising your divine given rights. And that evil force or energy that some call the devil. Sends malevolent entities or energies to keep you from moving forward on your divine path and knowing the truth in any matter.

So be aware of the energies that are sent in human form to block you and keep you distracted. Some of these energies can already be in your life posing as a friend, spouse, co-worker, or family member.

Also, make sure you are aware of the people that are around you and their true intentions towards you. It's always the one's you least expect that means you no good. So, pay close attention to people's actions and behavior towards you and others. They usually reveal unconsciously who they truly are at heart and how they feel about you and others. You cannot be ignoring the red flags or making excuses for people's behavior and actions. Believe them when they show you the first time who they are, their true colors, emotions, behavior, negative patterns, and hidden intentions.

If you don't you'll be blocking yourself and self-sabotaging yourself which keeps you stuck on the hamster wheel. If something does not feel right when you around certain individuals then act accordingly and remove yourself or remove them from having access to you. And don't be fool by their representative. Most people don't show you who they are at first, their representative is showcasing until they are ready to reveal their true self. So, pay attention to the subtle cues, such as their words, body language, facial expressions, tone of voice, or even their deliverance and posture. It'll reveal a lot on what the person is trying to hide, behind their representative mask.

So, use your discernment and intuition cause they will never lie to you. Always trust and believe in yourself, no matter how someone might try and gaslight or manipulate you into not trusting and second guessing your perception, judgement, and gut feelings. They are just trying to create internal conflict within you; to get you not

to trust yourself so they can block and hinder you. So, always trust in

yourself and your intuition it will never deceive or lie to you.

Spiritual Team

These are the celestial beings that some call angels, arch-angels, guardian angels, ascended masters, or ancestors. They are divine beings sent to protect, and help guide you along your divine life path. They been with you since the very beginning of your arrival to Earth, to help guide and assist you with fulfilling your soul contract and to guide you on your Soul's evolution.

You might cannot see them physically, but they are always there right by your side. You can sense their presence through subtle signs and feelings. Feeling a sense of calmness, peace, comfort, within you is a sign of their presence. Or a divine love and protection that you feel inside, that transcends this reality. Sometimes it's a smell that come out of nowhere in a sense; like smelling your grandma favorite perfume she used to wear or smelling the smoke from your grandpa cigar he used to smoke. Or you might see lights flicker or a knock that alerts you that their divine presence surrounds you.

When you become aware of self and energies and begin to tap into

and feel these unseen energies that surrounds you; you'll sense the

difference and know the presence that surrounds you. And when

you start to open yourself up to wanting to communicate or reach

out to them, you'll begin to see little orbs, which are also them.

Sometimes you just see the orbs while you driving and its them

alerting you they are near and with you.

So, no need to be afraid your divine spiritual team works for you

and want what is best for you. They speak to you through different

divination tools, dreams, and various of other forms of symbolisms

and synchronicities. But you must be aware, open, and receptive to

their presence, and have the eye to see, so you don't miss the signs

they send you.

Because they have always been protecting and guiding you, whether you are aware of it or not. They are known to help you fight your spiritual battles here in the physical and astral realms. Also, they speak to you through your intuition or your meditative state. They alert you of danger lurking nearby, but will never allow something to happen to you. For example, you're leaving home but you can't find something you need, and you're running late. That's them stalling you so you don't run into the danger that is occurring. It could have been an accident but those extra minutes or time it took for you looking for your lost item or keys saved you from being involved in the accident. So, make sure you are listening and paying attention to them.

They are a part of your inner navigation system working to guide you and keep you protected on your divine path. They were assigned to you by the Divine and yourself before this incarnation to help you in this human experience. And you get new ones added at each new level you reach or need to defeat.

They don't play about you and will shut it down about you. So, send them love and gratitude, and other offerings by burning ancestral money or lighting a candle in their memory. And you can even set up an altar in their memory. You can add their favorite thing, food, or drink. Cause they put in work for you and will go to war for you.

Divination Tools

Divination tools are used for a variety of reasons. For example, to gain insight or clarity on situations or current circumstances, and/or people, places, and things. To foresee or foretell and events that has happened or will happen. They are also used but not limited to, communicating with your spirit guides, your higher selves, and to help you with navigating uncertainties. Some tools used are tarot cards, oracle cards, pendulums, numerology, astrology, animals, and angel numbers, etc.

Also, keep in mind everyone's messages differs from others. After all, this is your spiritual team or the Divine speaking directly to you using these energies. Overall, these practices are a form of energetic communication and connecting with your intuition.

Our ancient ancestors used these tools for a variety of reasons but most importantly to seek higher knowledge, wisdom and understanding. These tools are very sacred. So, you cannot seek readings and divination guidance from just anyone. Have discernment and be sure you can trust that person. Because some people can mislead you, and tap into your energy and start manipulating you and your life.

Also have discernment when you are utilizing these tools yourself. These tools are just a stepping stone once you fully tap into yourself and gain self-trust and self-belief. You might find yourself not needing some or none of these tools any longer because you'll be able to navigate and discern energies, situations, and circumstances yourself by following your intuition.

Angel Numbers

Angel numbers are a sequence of numbers (123, 333, 1111, 444, 555), used as a communication tool for the Divine and your divine spiritual team to communicate with you. They often appear in patterns of three or four digits. Each number holds a different meaning. And these angel numbers can be seen in random places. They can be seen on a clock, a receipt, billboard and/or license plates, etc. These messages are offered as reminders for self-reflection, and to trust your intuition, or changes/transitions occurring, spiritual growth and enlightenment, or directionality on your life's journey. These numbers can also offer insight on your current situation, or as encouragement, and your connection to your divine spiritual team.

However, you have to be open to receiving these divine messages. By paying attention to your thoughts and feelings at the time of seeing the angel numbers. Also, your surroundings and current situations can play a part to what the message is trying to convey to you. But the signs are always present you just have to be aware and open to them. And everyone's messages differs from others. Also, keep in mind that each number carries its own meaning and vibration. And sometimes you have to simplify the number to get a better interpretation of the message. But usually, the angel numbers messages is quite clear and evident.

In addition, animals hold a spiritual meaning and symbolism as well, and convey spiritual messages that come from your divine spiritual team when they cross your path or when seen on oracle cards. For example, seeing a blue jay bird could mean bold expression, speaking your truth, confidence, inner strength, courage, or communication from a deceased loved one, and guidance/protection. But to inner-stand these messages you must be open to receiving them. Also, keep in mind everyone's messages differs from others.

Heaven aka New Earth

This is the dimension the Divine elevates you to, after your resurrection. After, the Divine, has healed, renewed and restored you. From all the traumas, and scars you endured while being in the underworld amongst demons and all of that toxicity. If you made it to this level than you have reached a pivotal point in your life's journey, and you have survived and recovered from the hell you have just walked through.

Now, you are in the grace of the Divine, in your natural state, sitting on your throne. You made the choice to liberate and save yourself. Now, you are enjoying the fruits of life. You carry no shame or guilt for loving the wrong people, for you were on divine assignment. And you learned so much in that period of time about yourself and others. And you are nothing like the people you were once surrounded by. You have used those horrible experiences as invaluable lessons, deep introspection, significant self-growth, personal transformation, and deep healing. You have come very far on your life's journey, and you have slayed many of demons, including big ones. And your heart is still pure and intact. They failed their mission and now living in a constant, consistent mental state of hell for trying to come up against a Chosen One. And you, on the other hand, are living in the Promised Land, serving out your divine purpose. You tried to teach and show them this new way of living to no avail. And that's okay, you did your best.

But before the Divine could elevate you, the Divine had to expose you to everyone's heart around you. So, you will know who can come with you, and those you must love from a distant and leave behind. Because everyone can't come to the Promised Land. And elevation will always require separation.

You are now able to enjoy healthy connections and experiences with healthy people of the same energy signature and vibration you carry.

The Divine and your divine spiritual team are so proud of you. You are continuously evolving and learning. While still being protected and guided. And you are highly favored and loved by your divine spiritual team and the Divine. Now, it's Freedom Time Chosen Ones, and Congratulations! You have conquered the unconquerables.

I reclaim and call back all my power and energy with DIVINE force and DIVINE care.

-Goddess Ravin Nicole

www.ingramcontent.com/pod-product-compliance
Lightning Source LLC
LaVergne TN
LVHW051423080426
835508LV00022B/3211